WELCOME
TO
COLOR ME BOTANICALS I
AN ADULT COLORING BOOK

PLEASE VISIT OUR WEBSITE FOR MORE INFORMATION ON NEW DESIGNS,
BOOKS AND PRINTS AT
WWW.BOTANICALARTDESIGNS.COM

COPYRIGHT © 2015 BY CAROL MENNIG
ALL RIGHTS RESERVED.
ISBN: 1511881194
ISBN-13: 978-1511881197

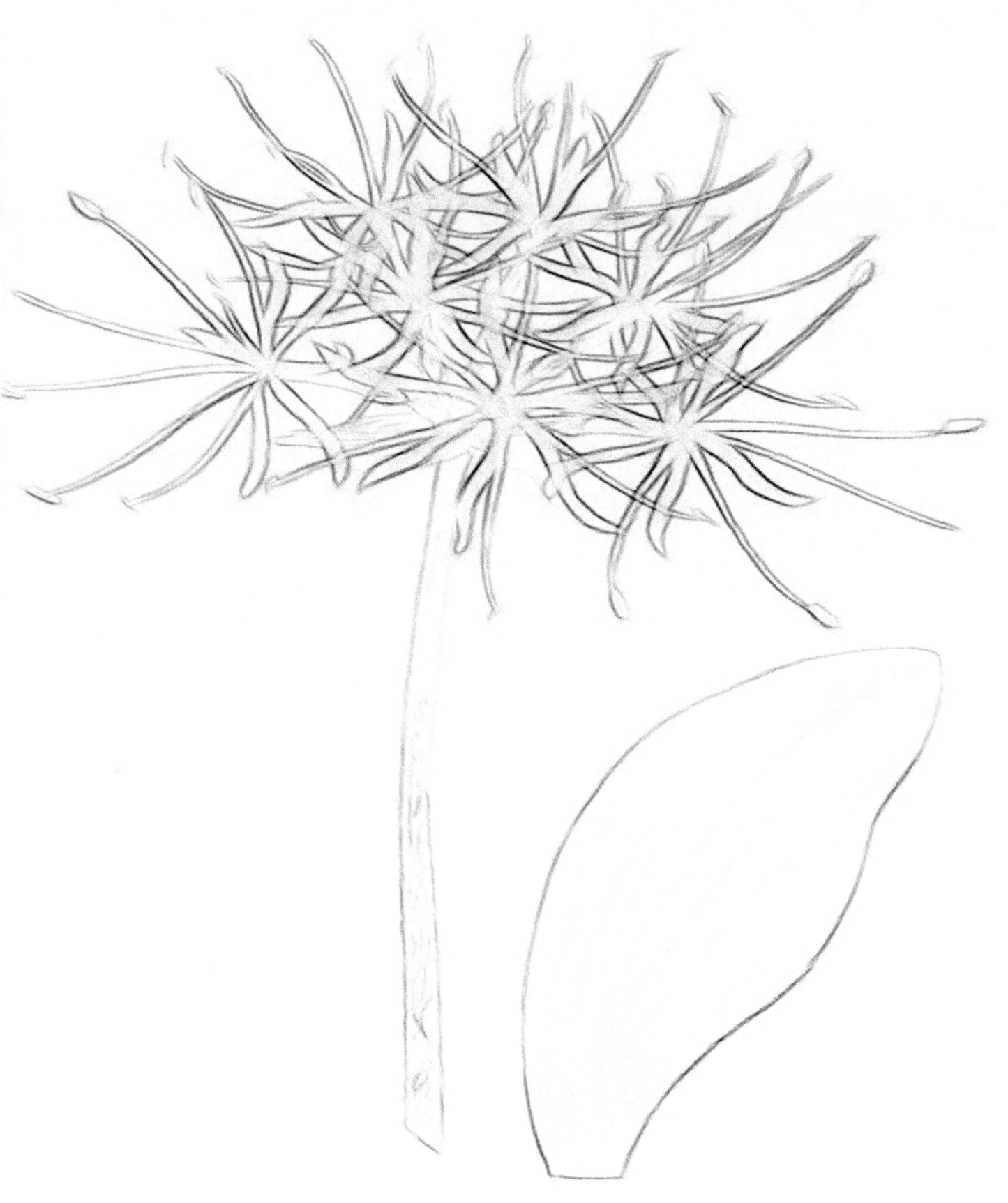

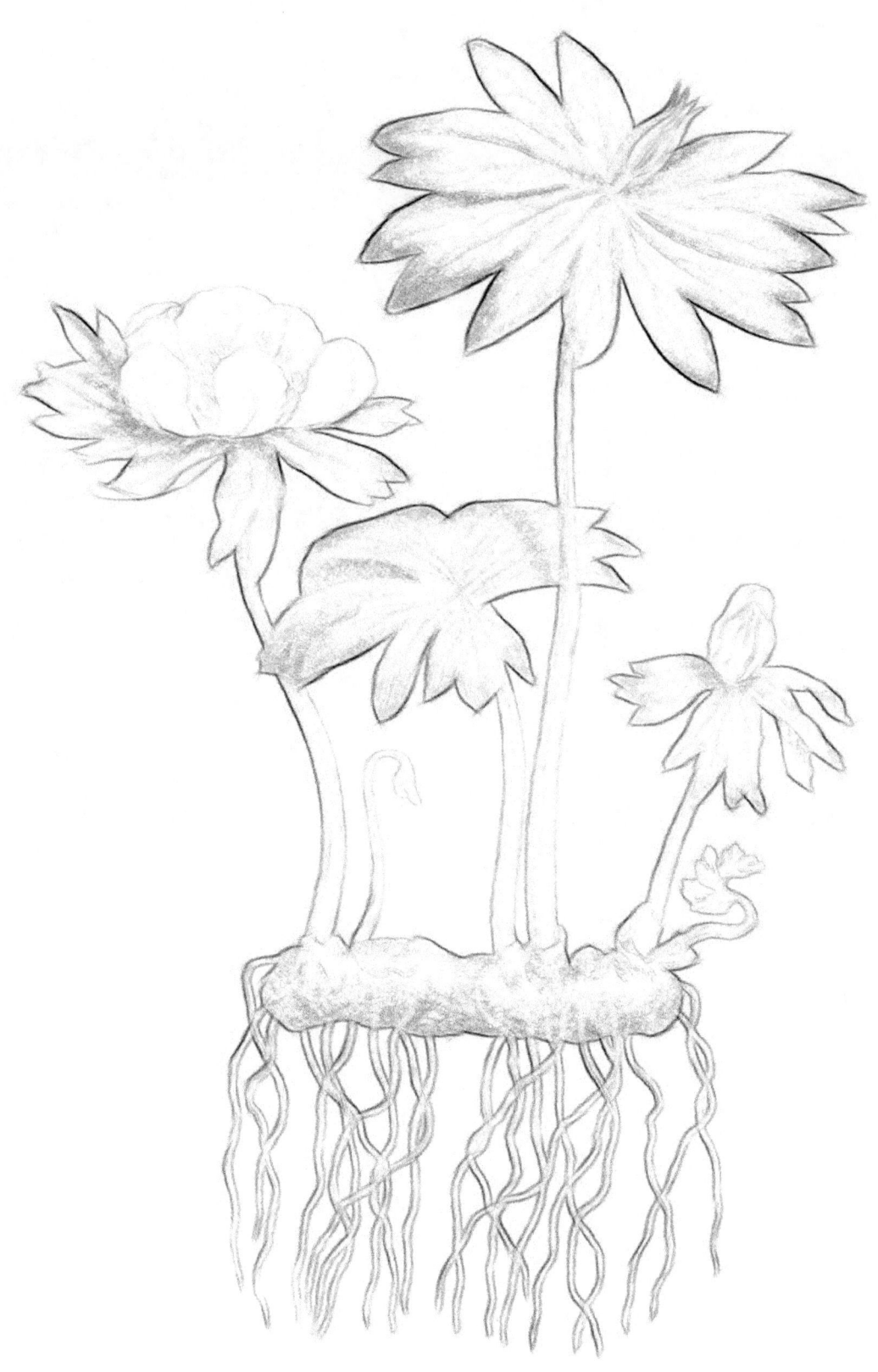

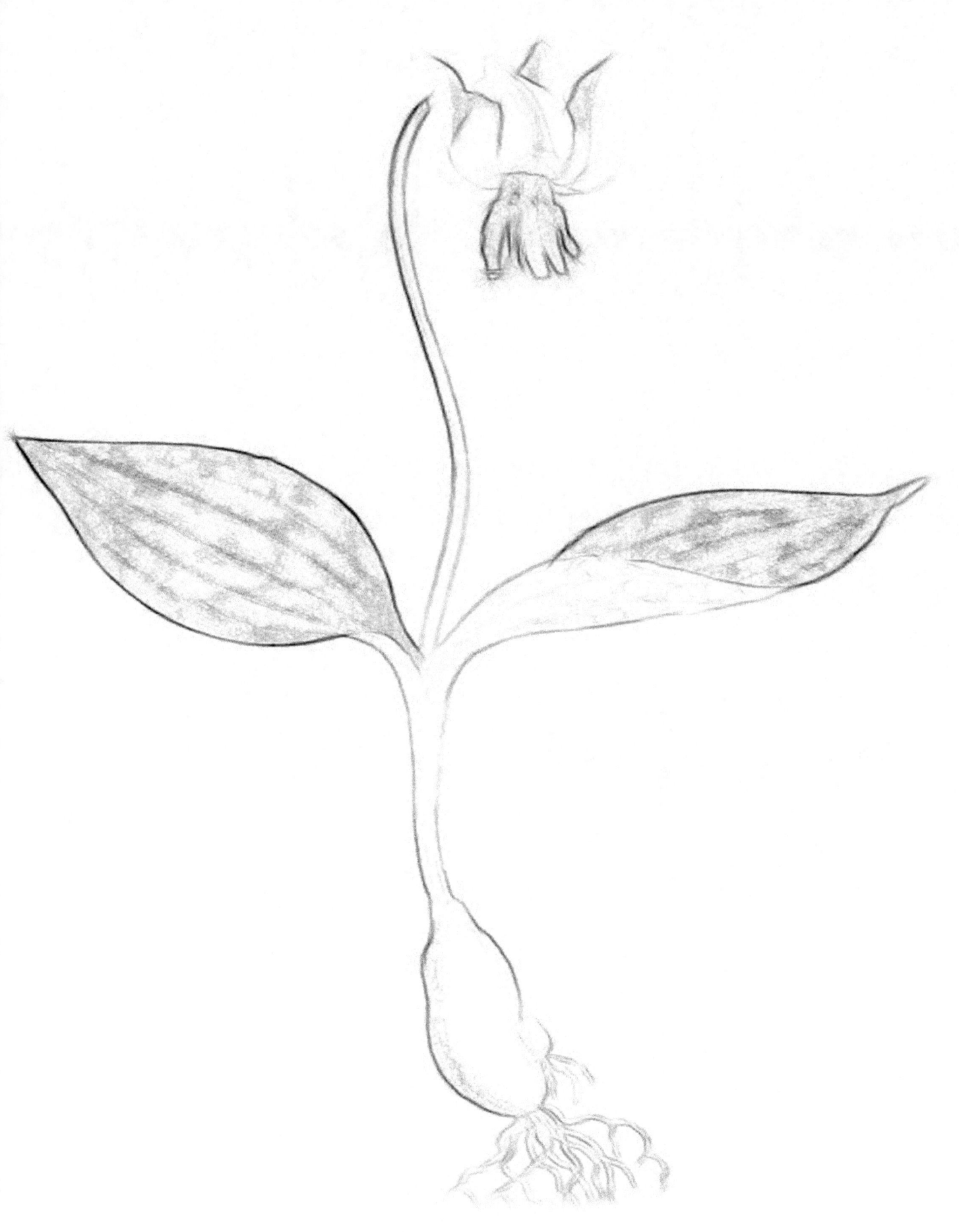

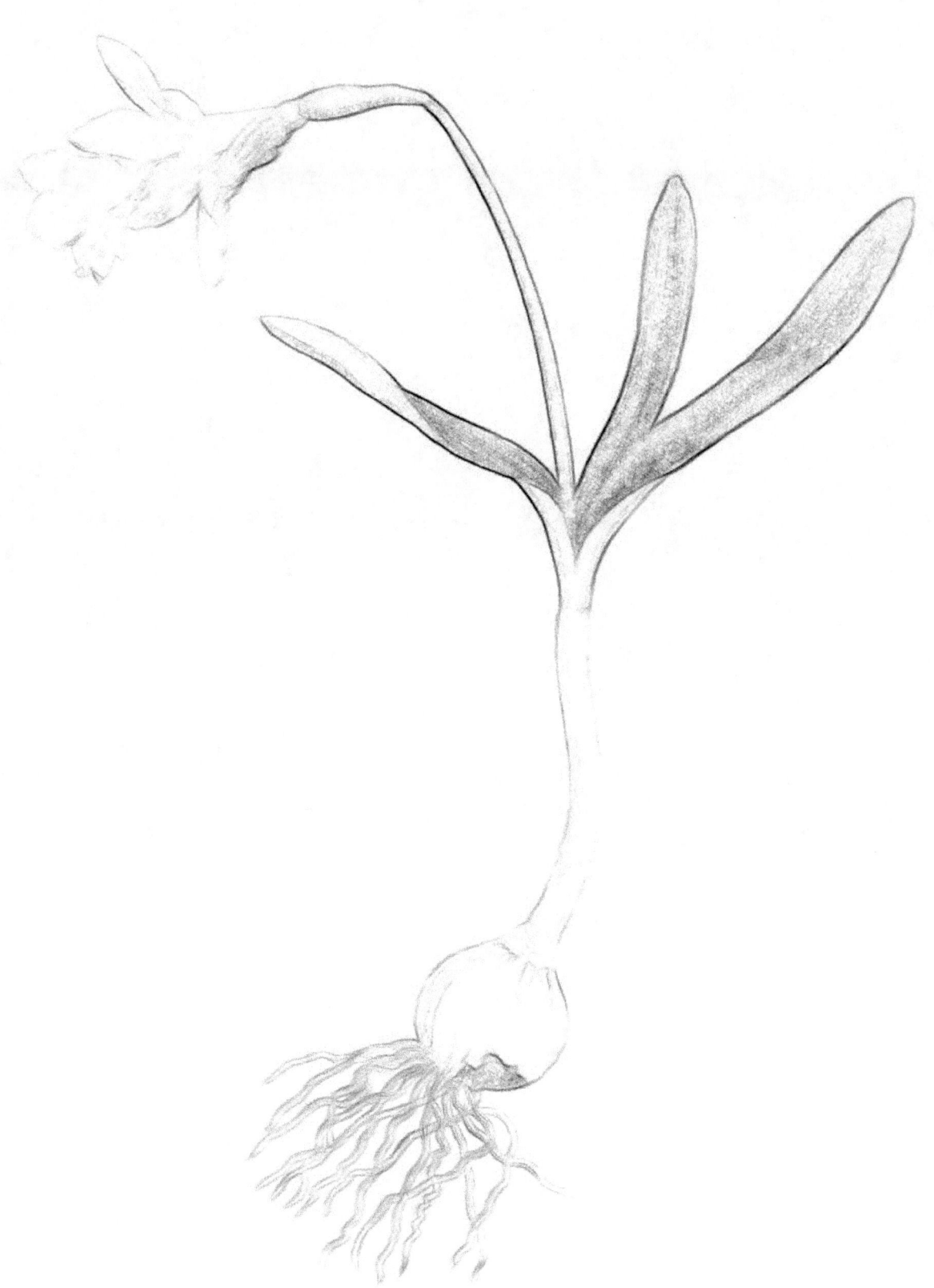

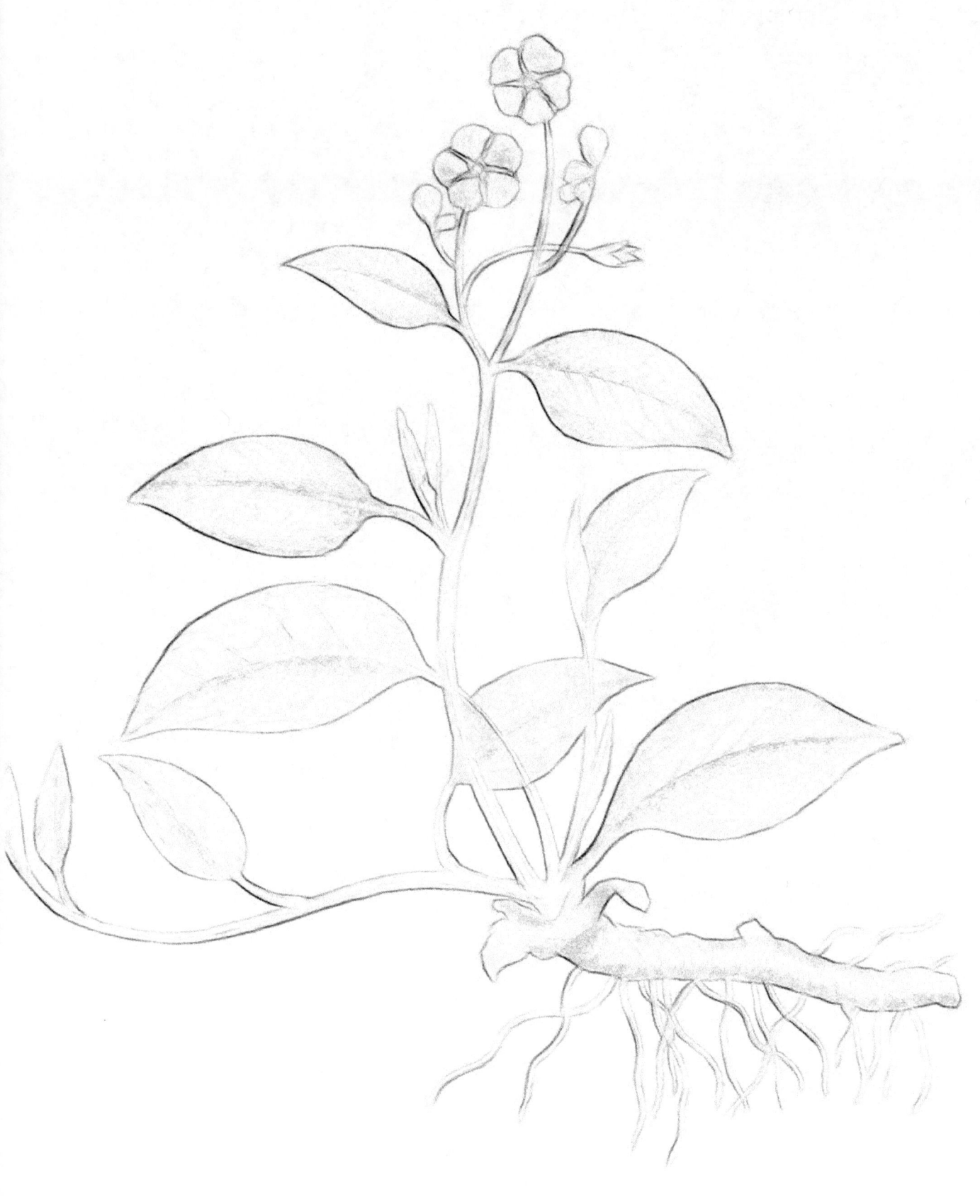

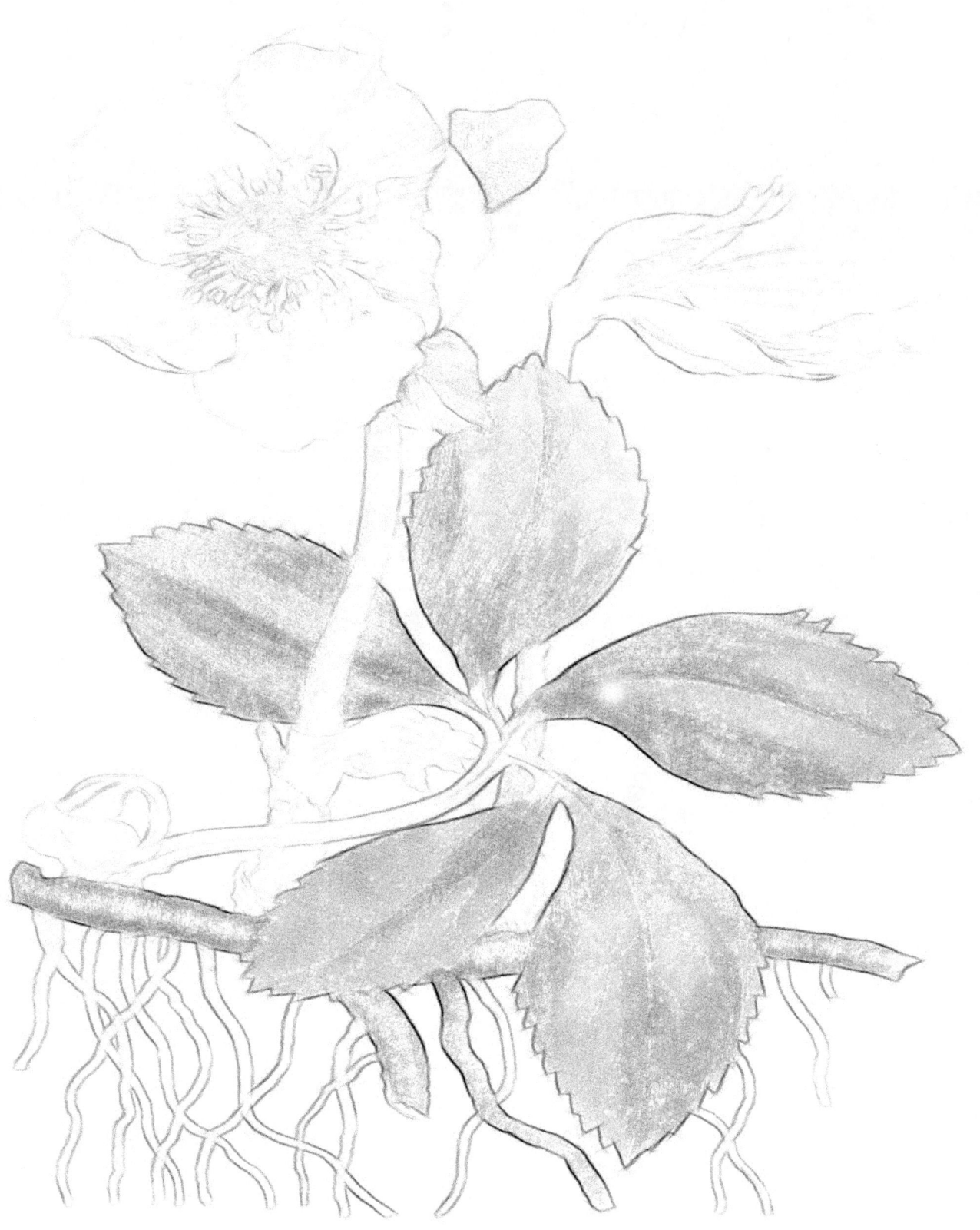

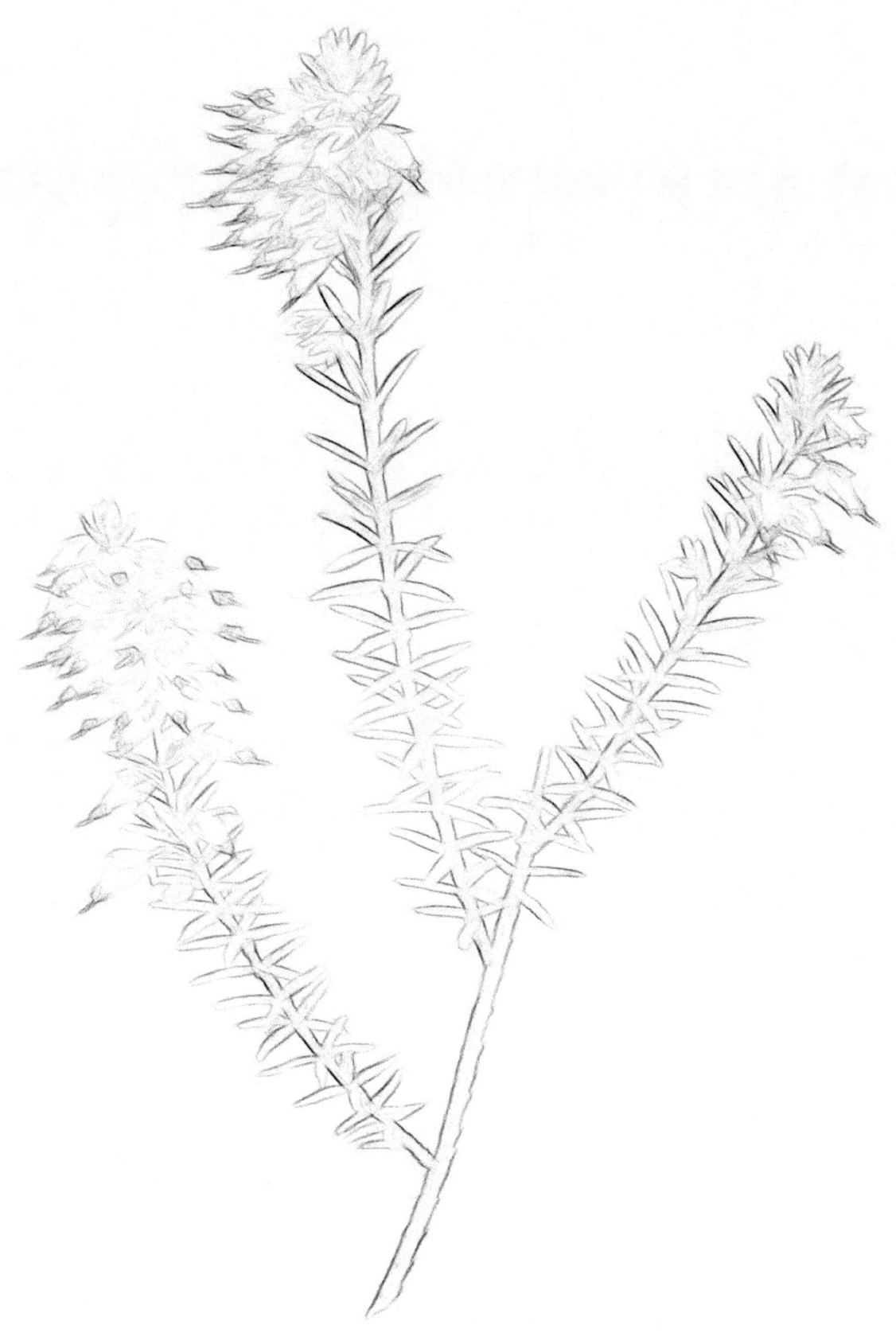

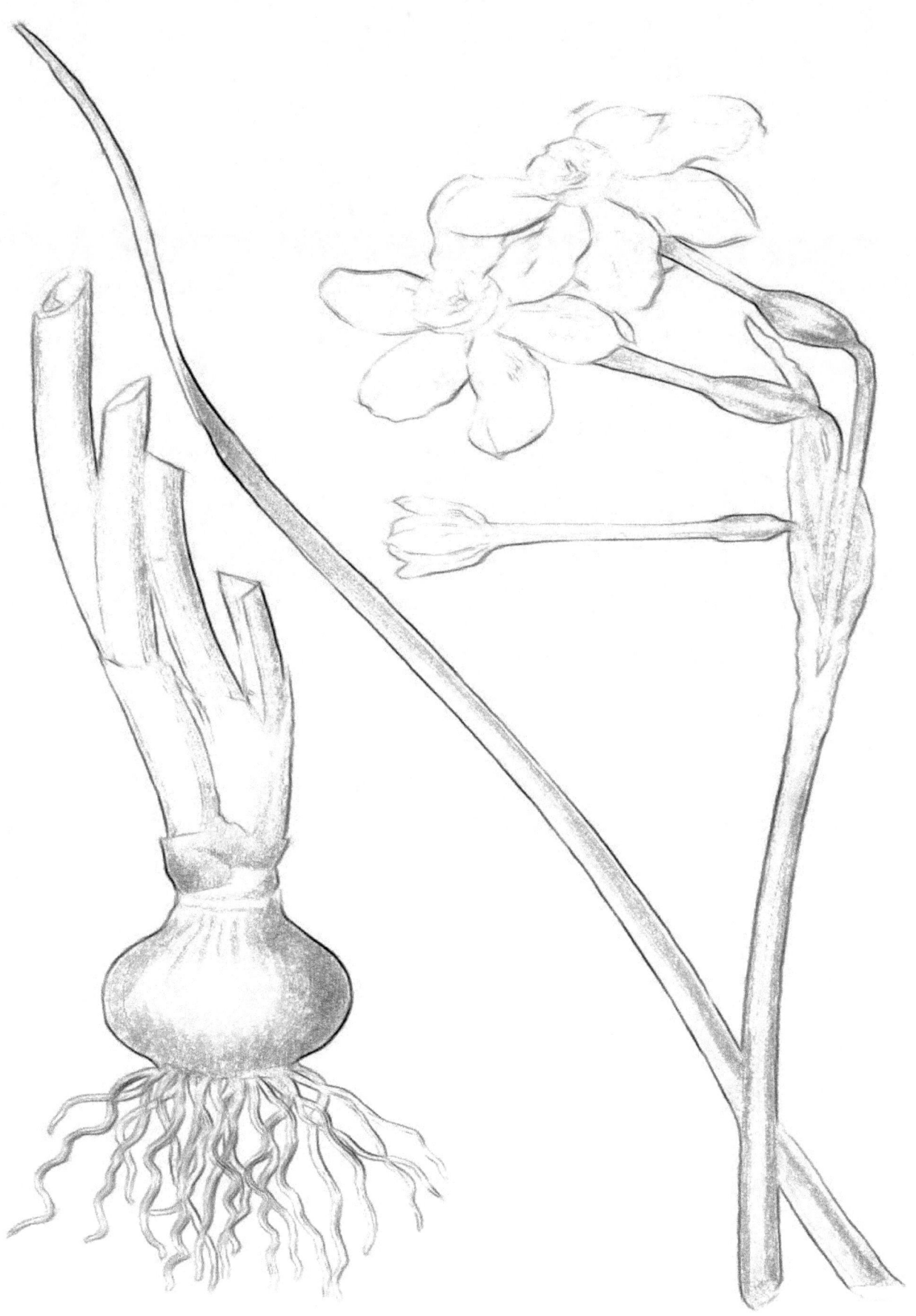

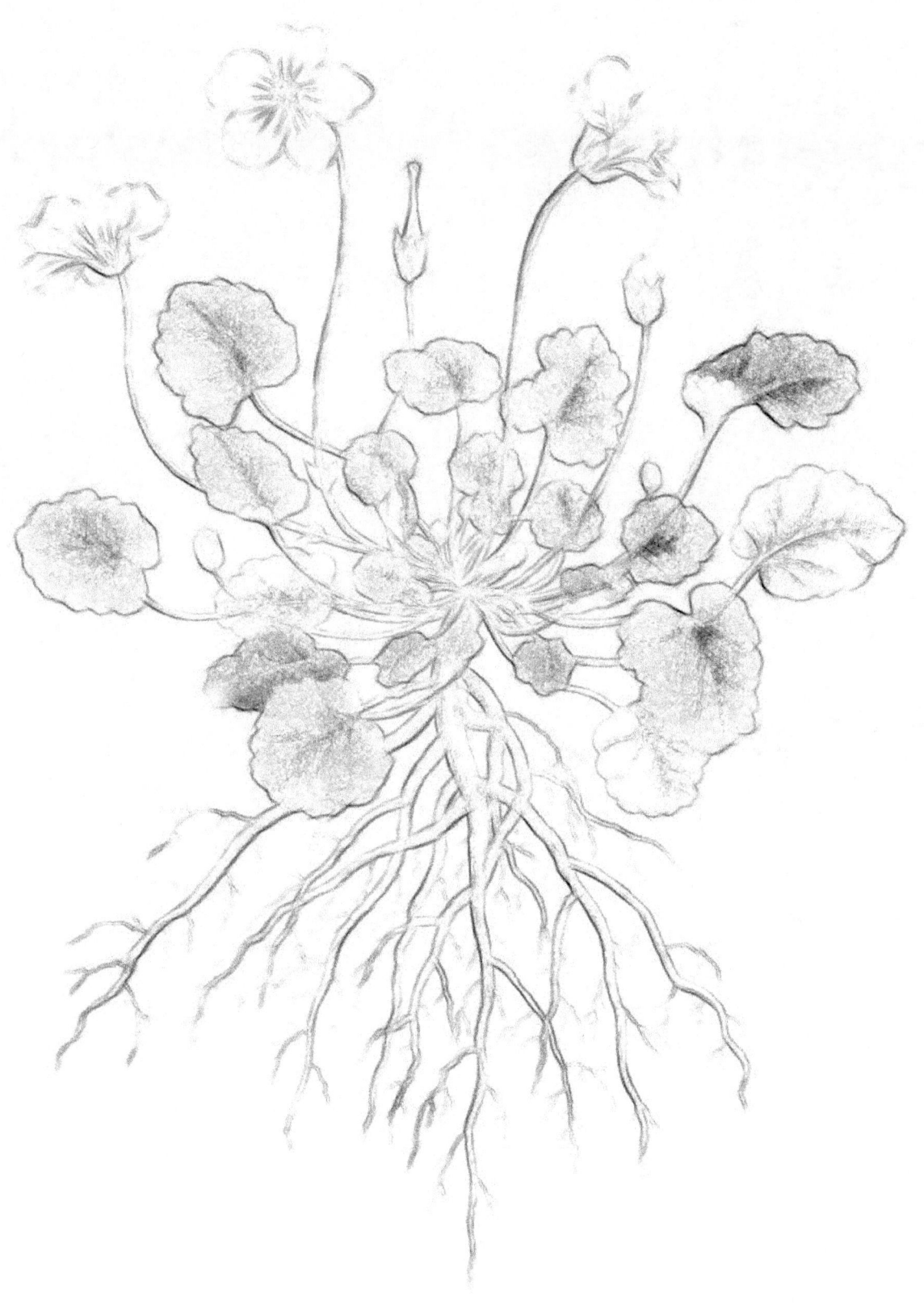

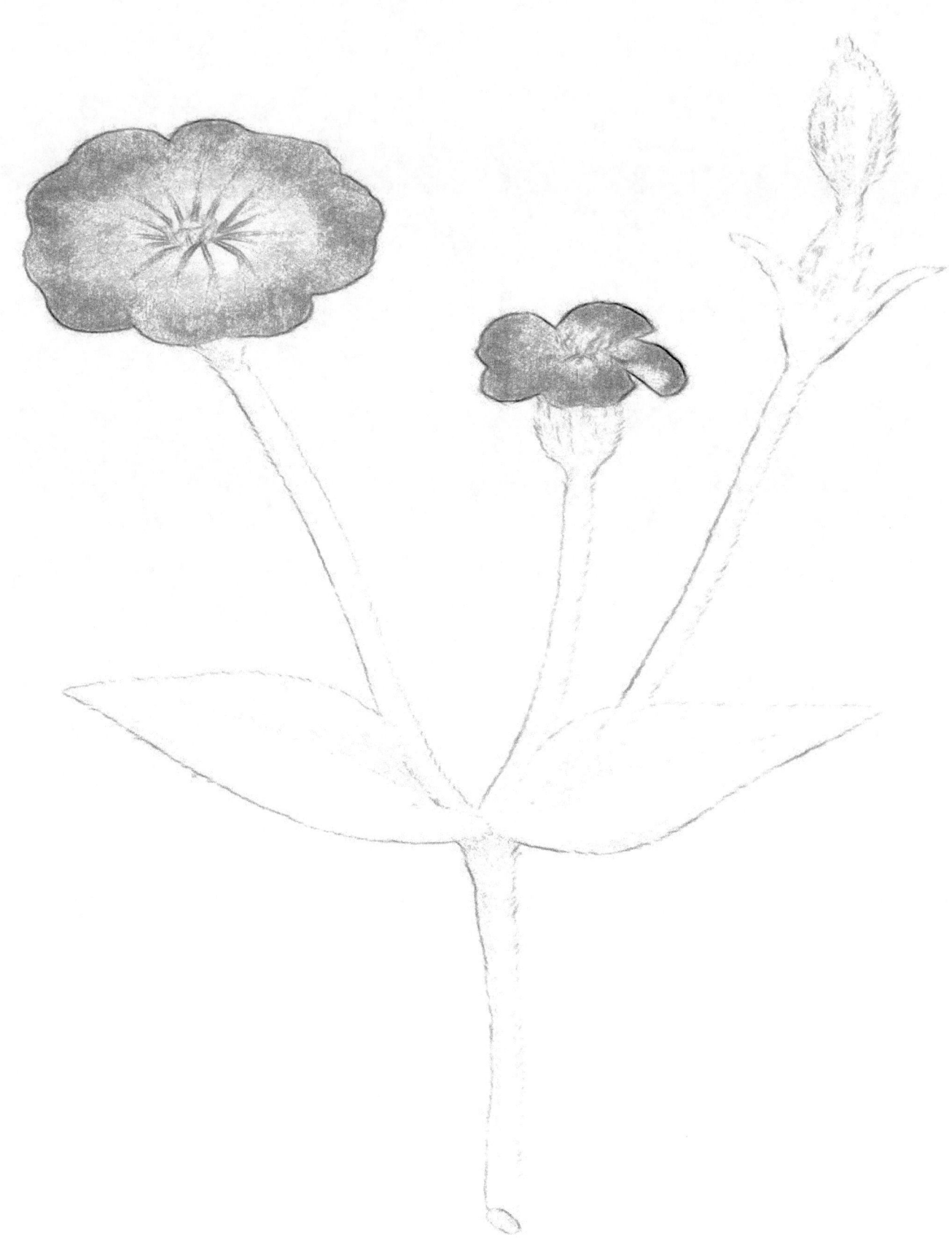

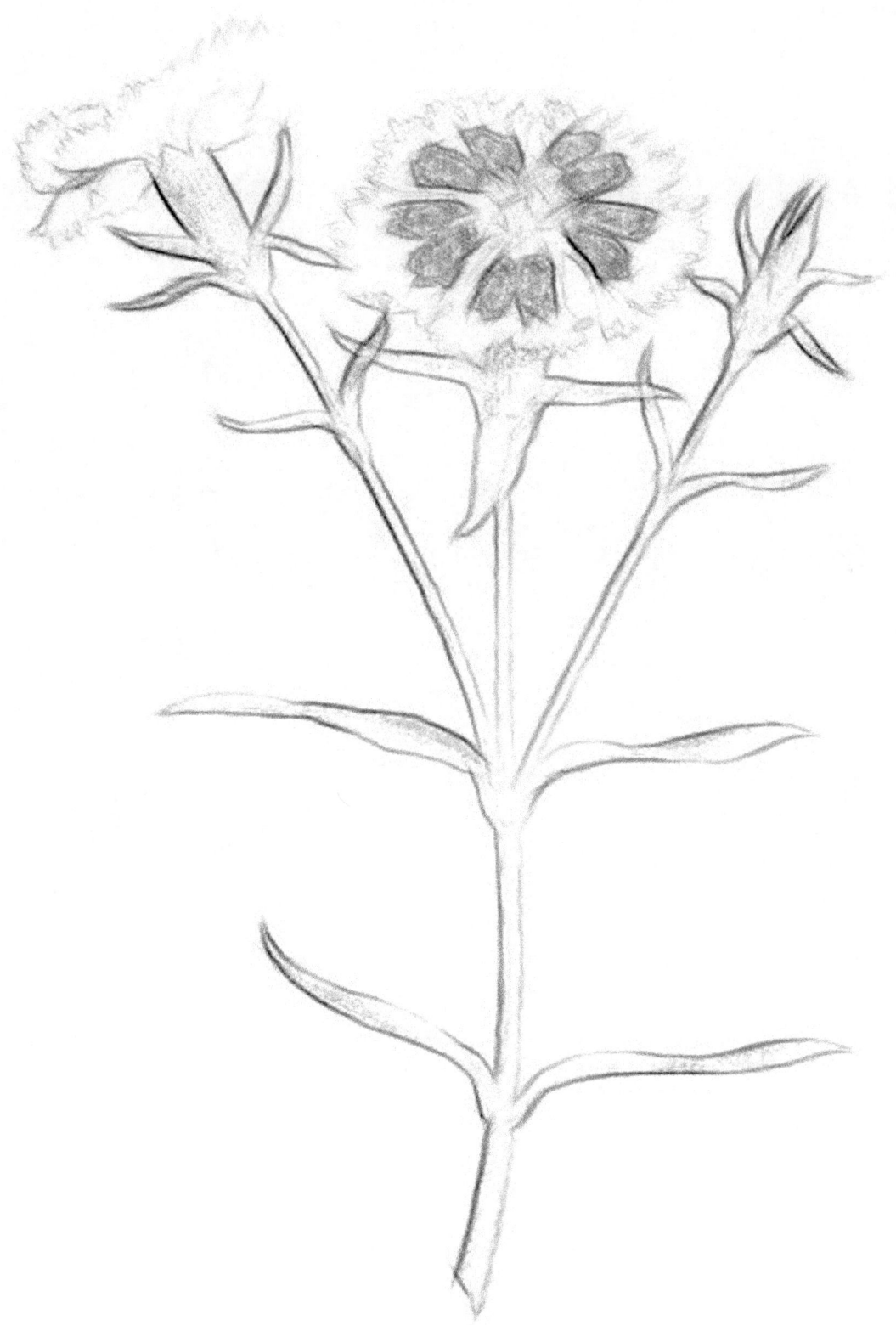

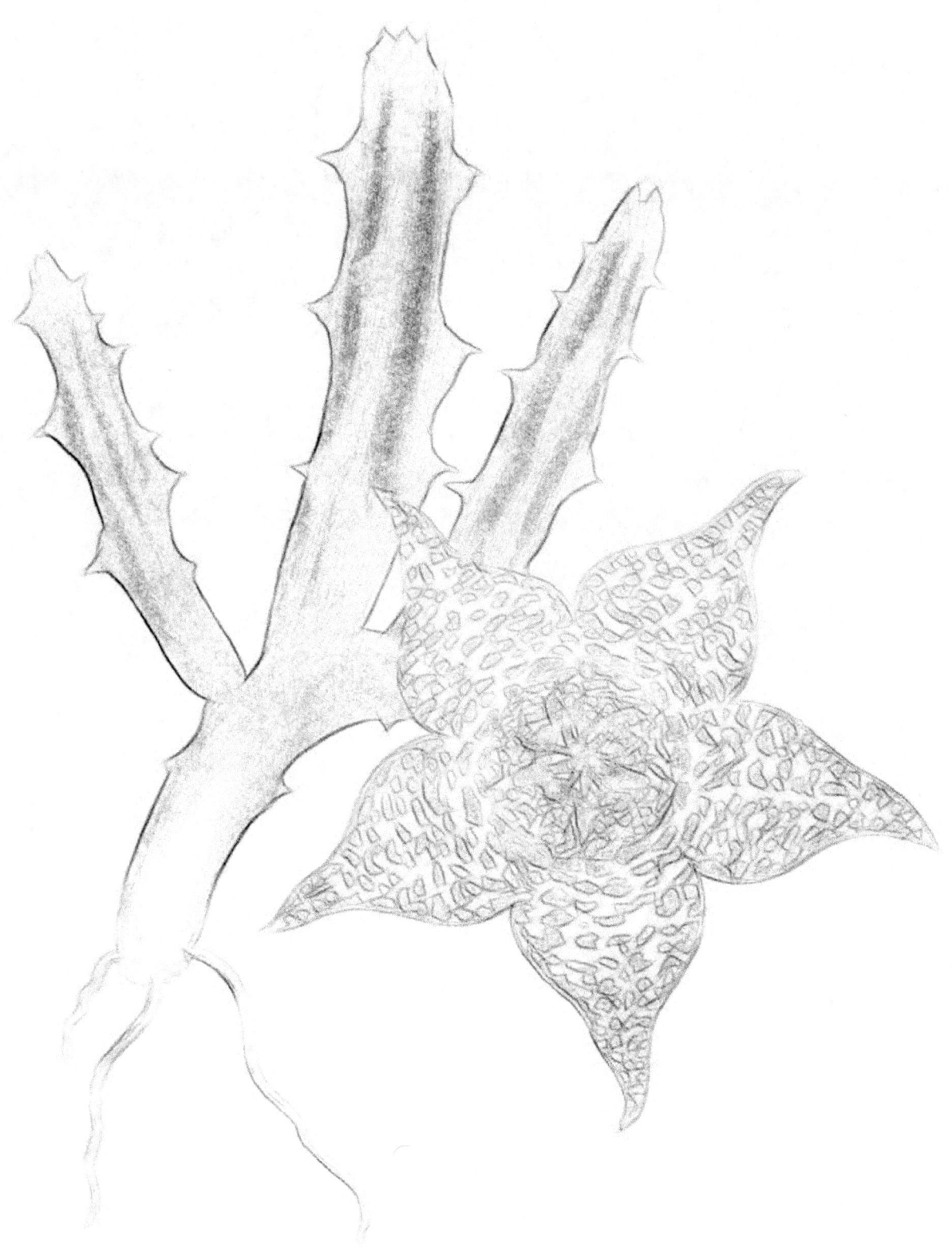

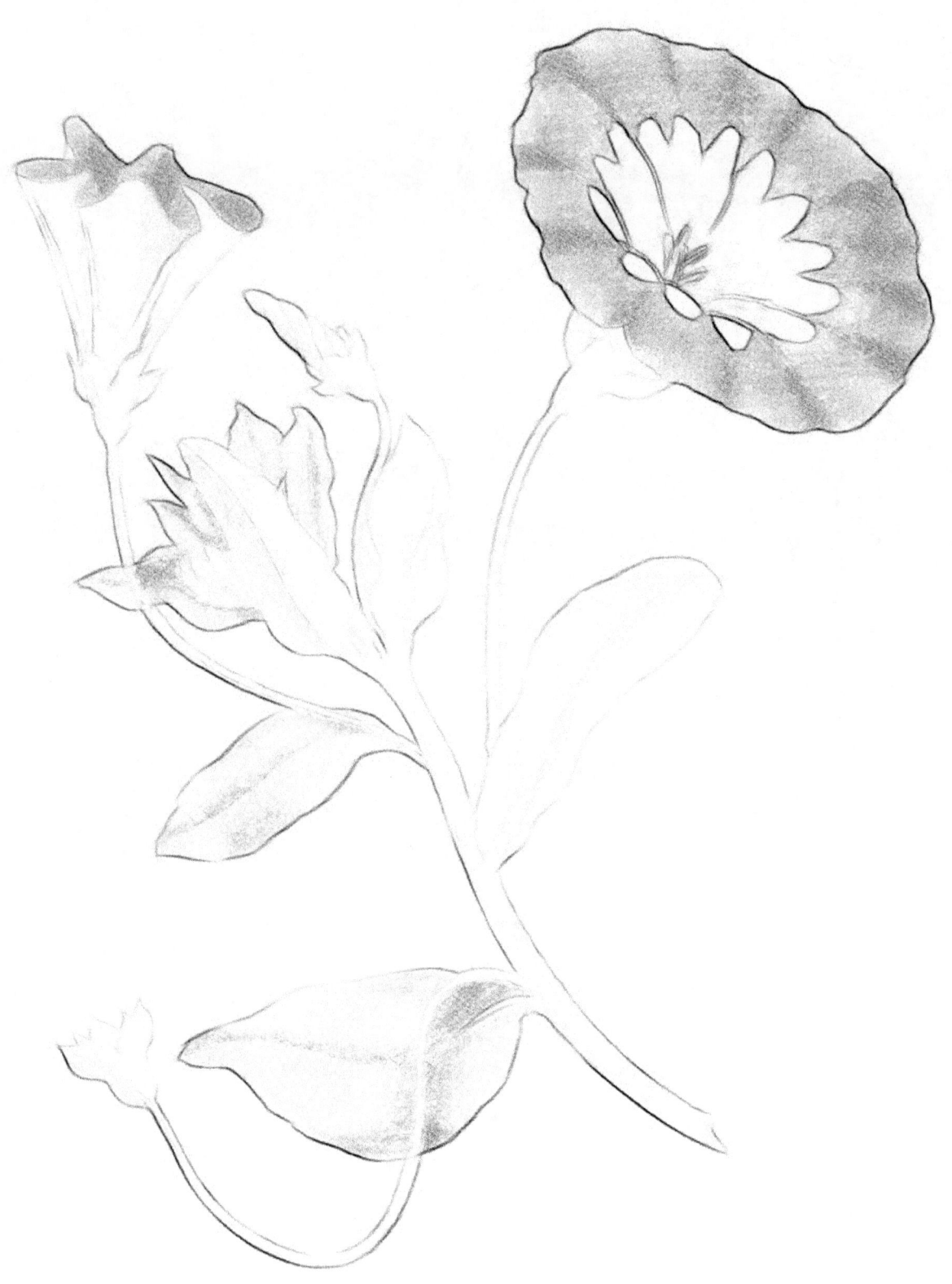

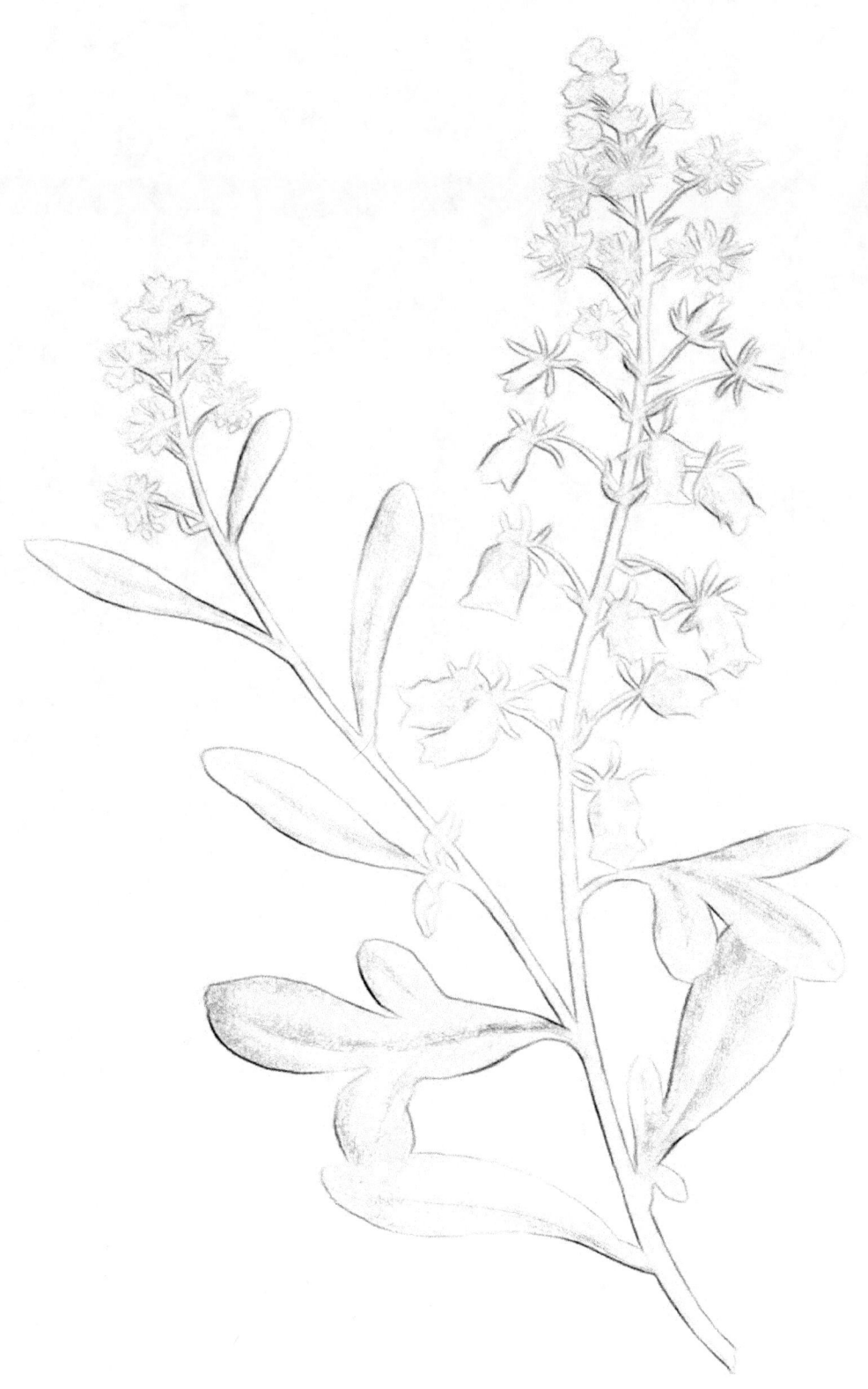

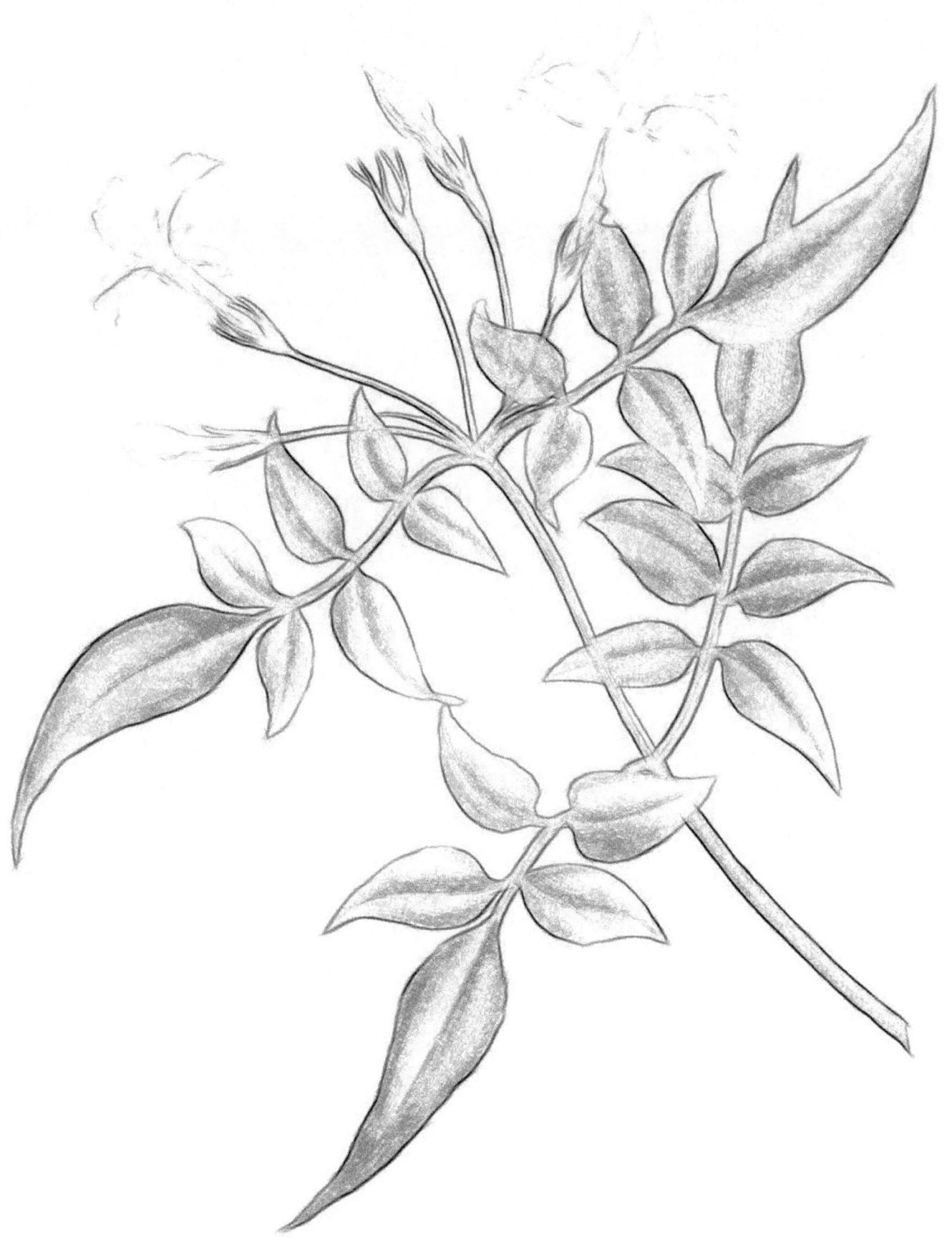

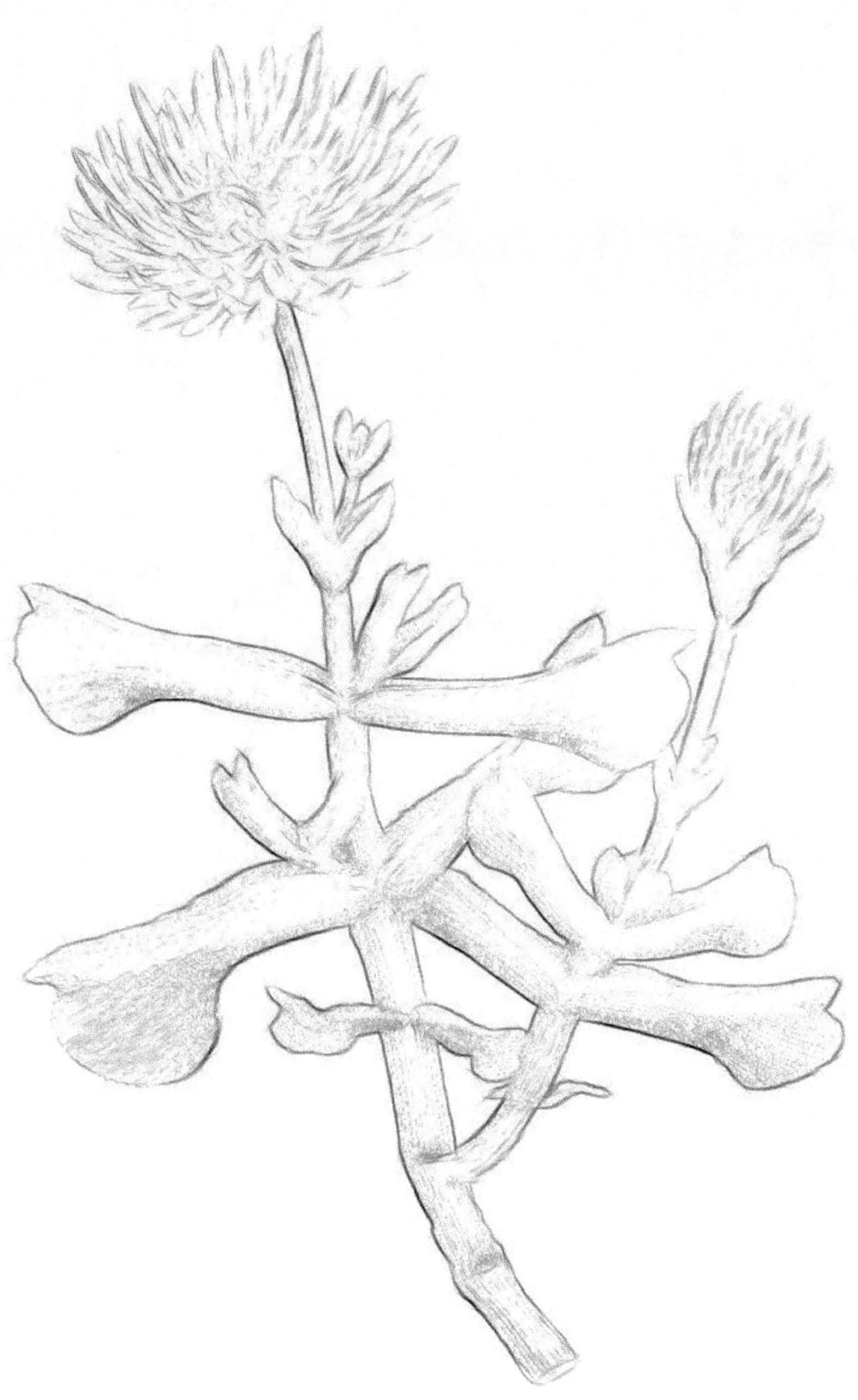

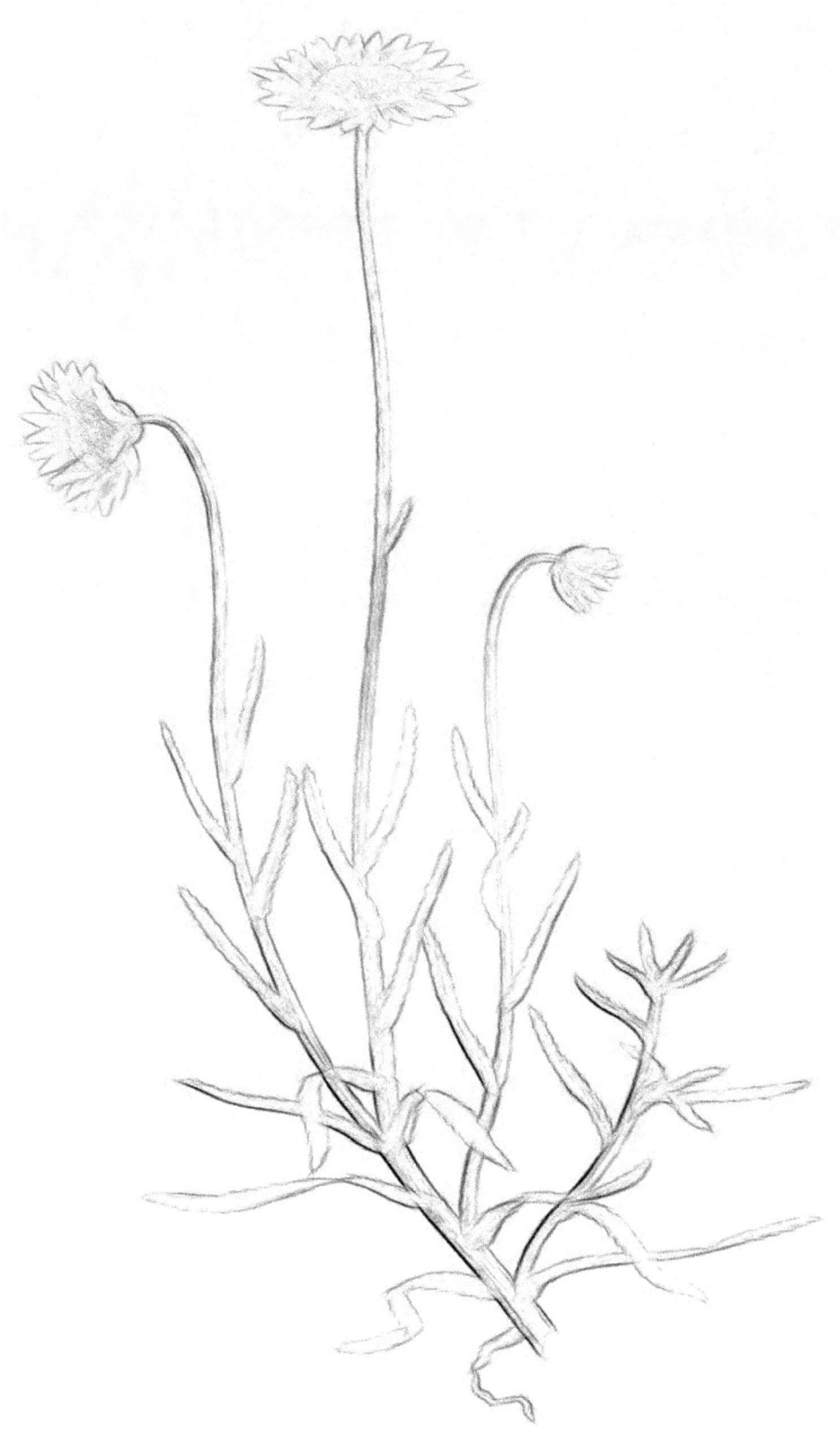

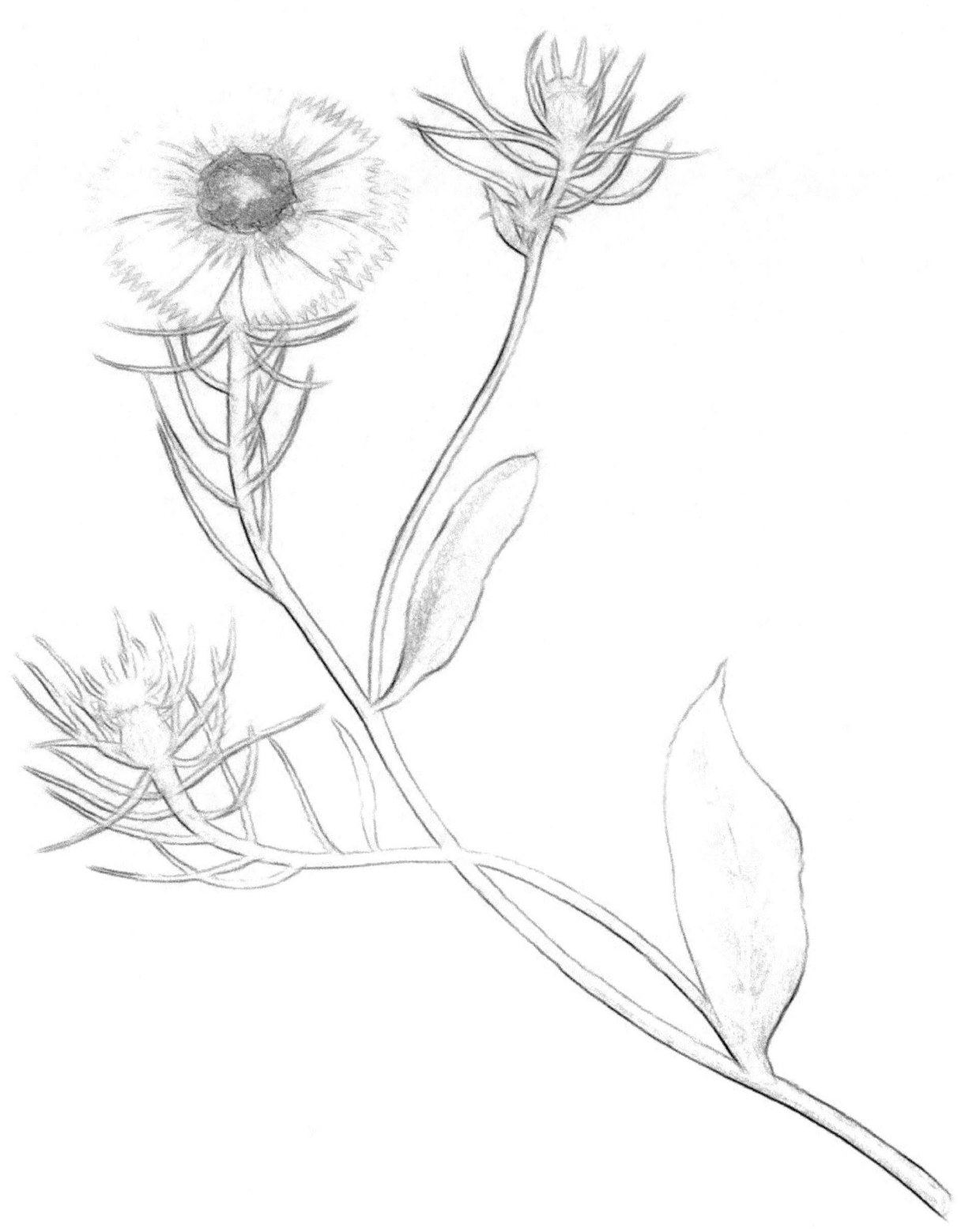

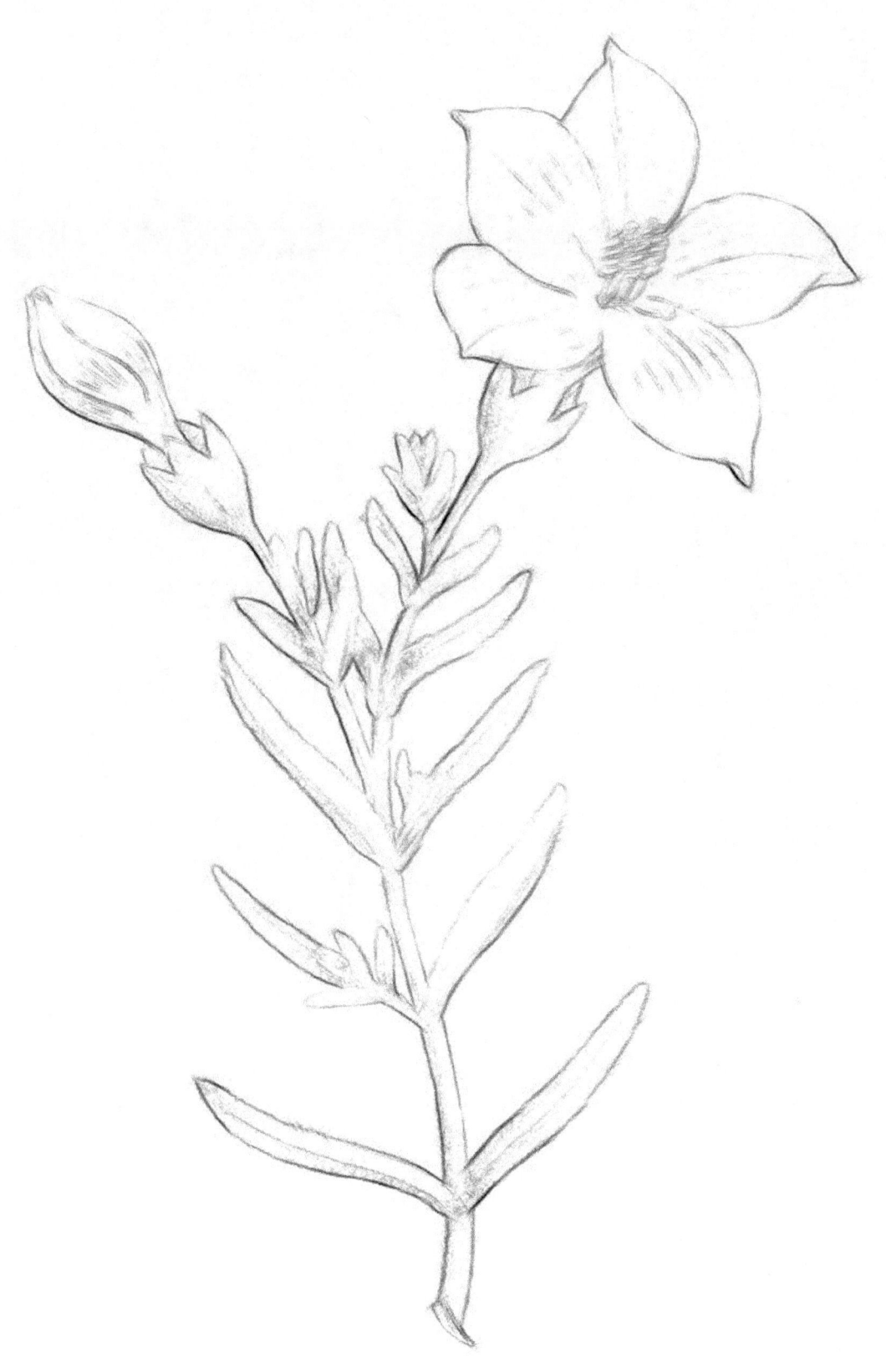

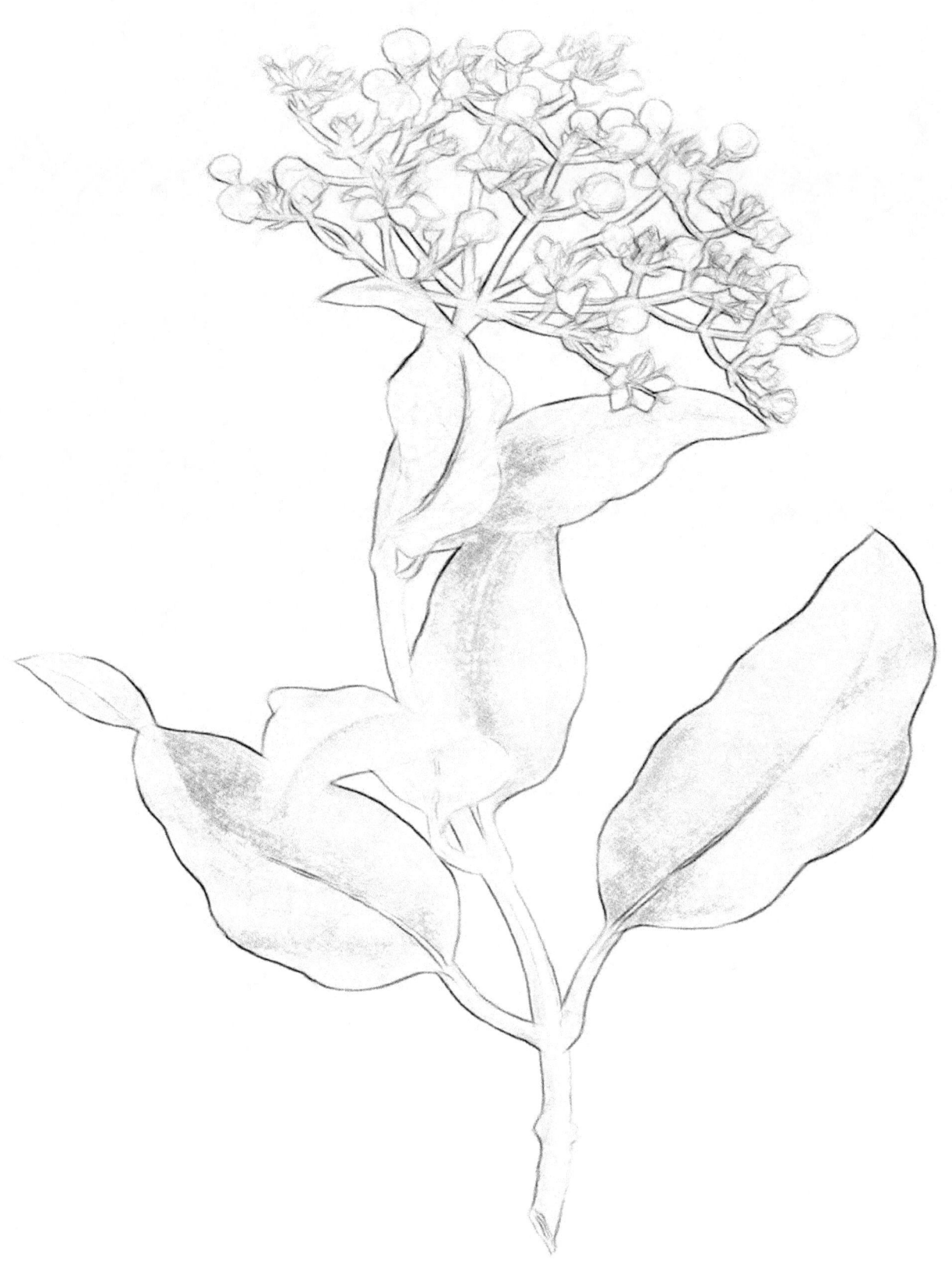

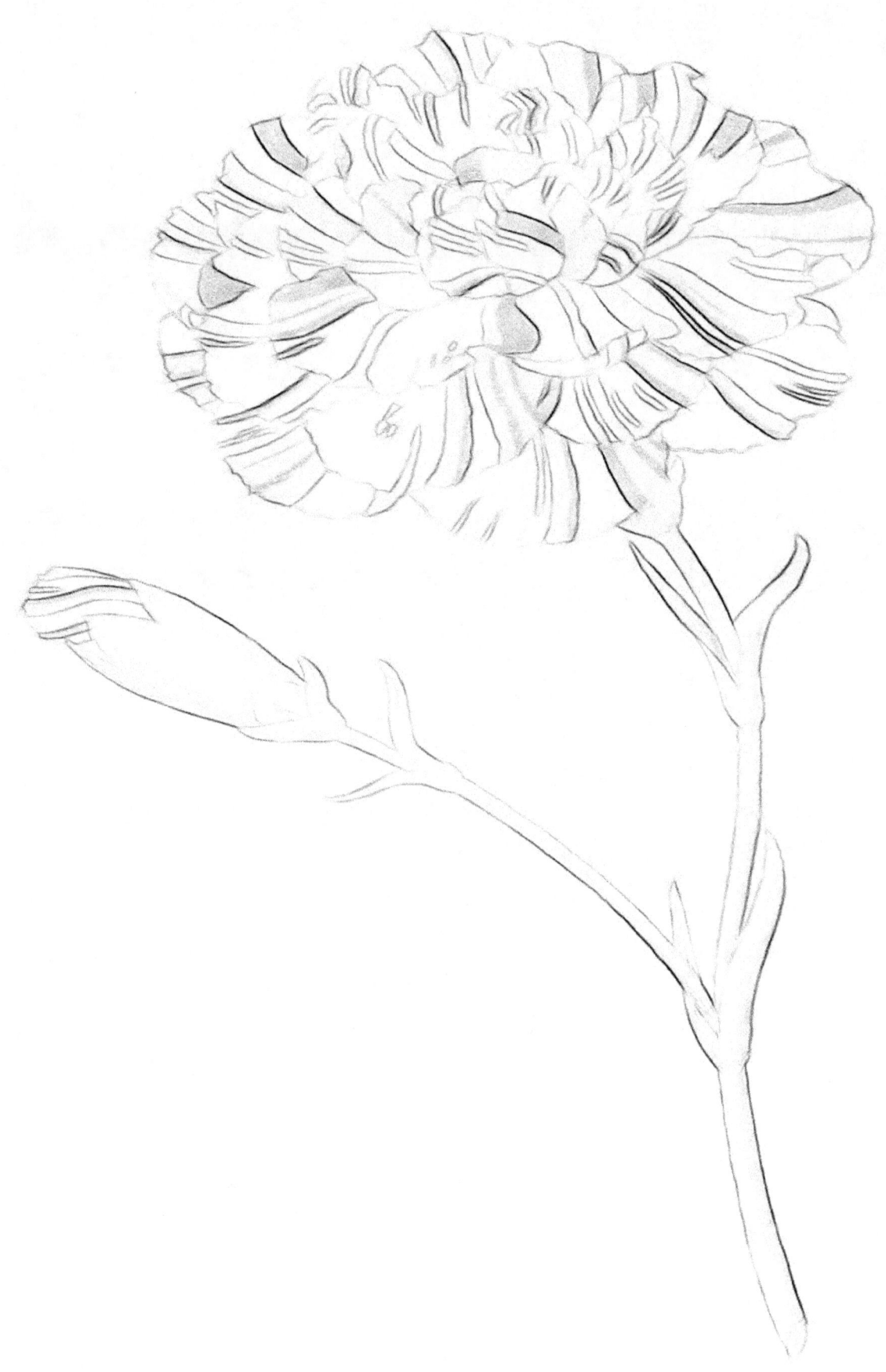

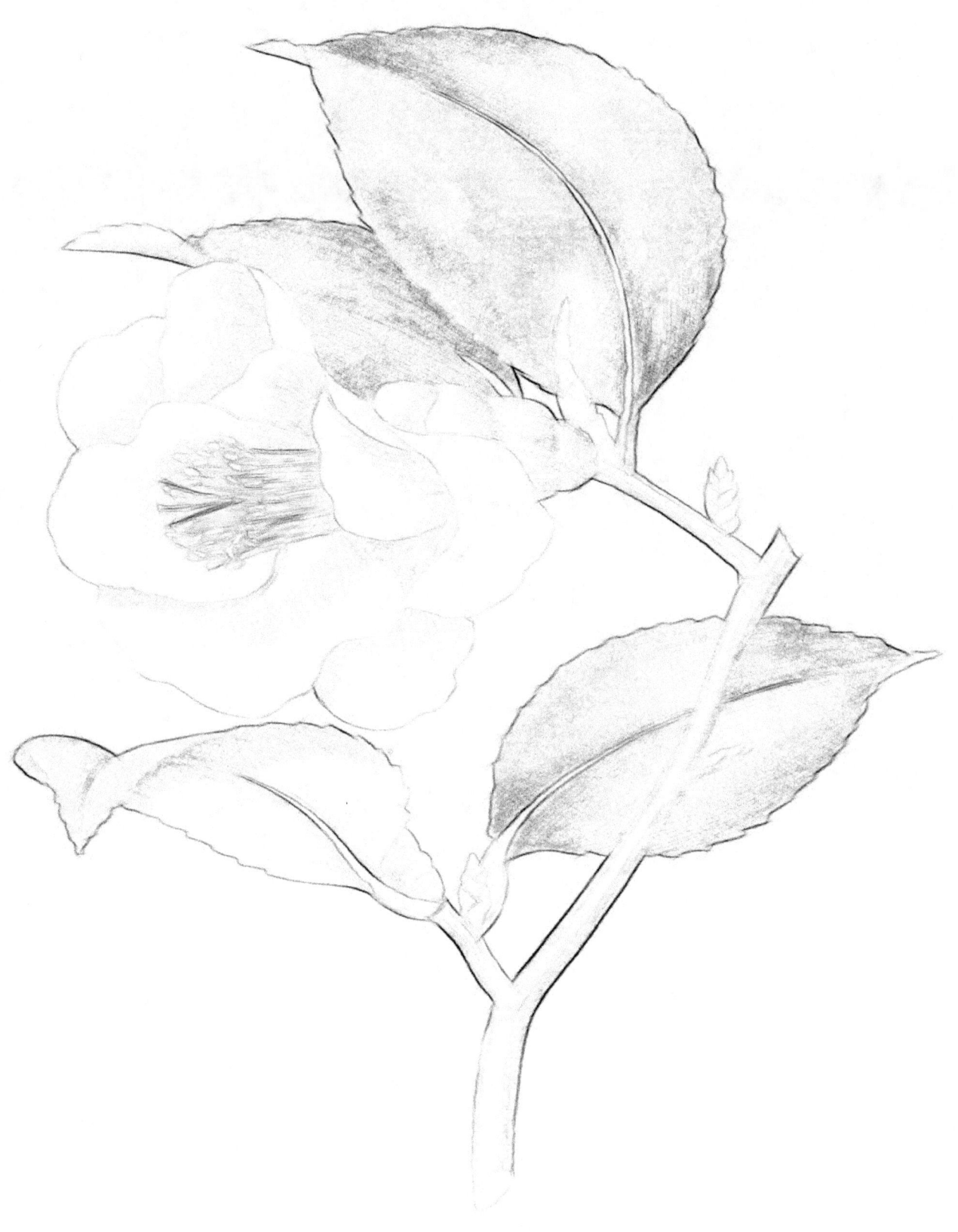

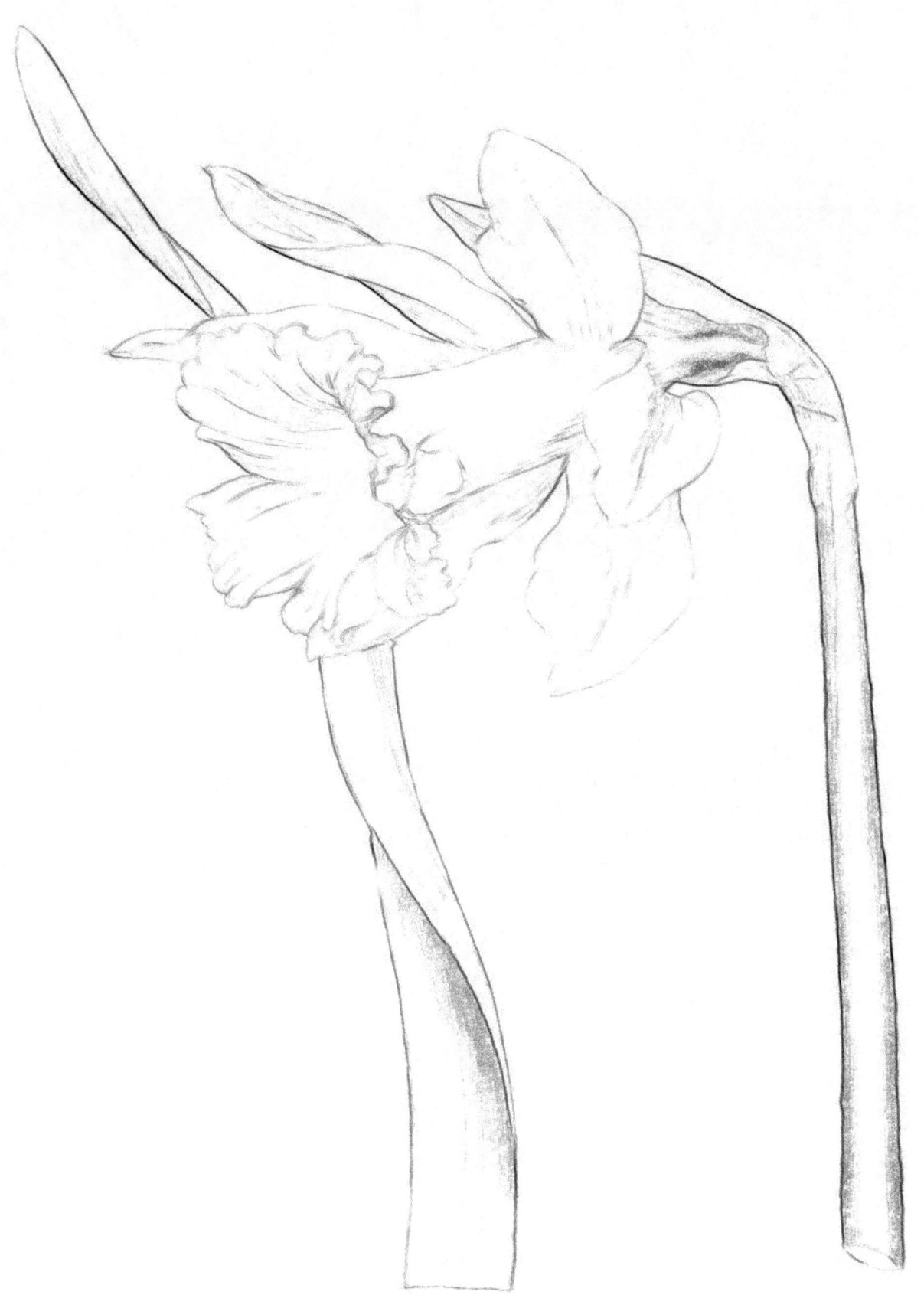

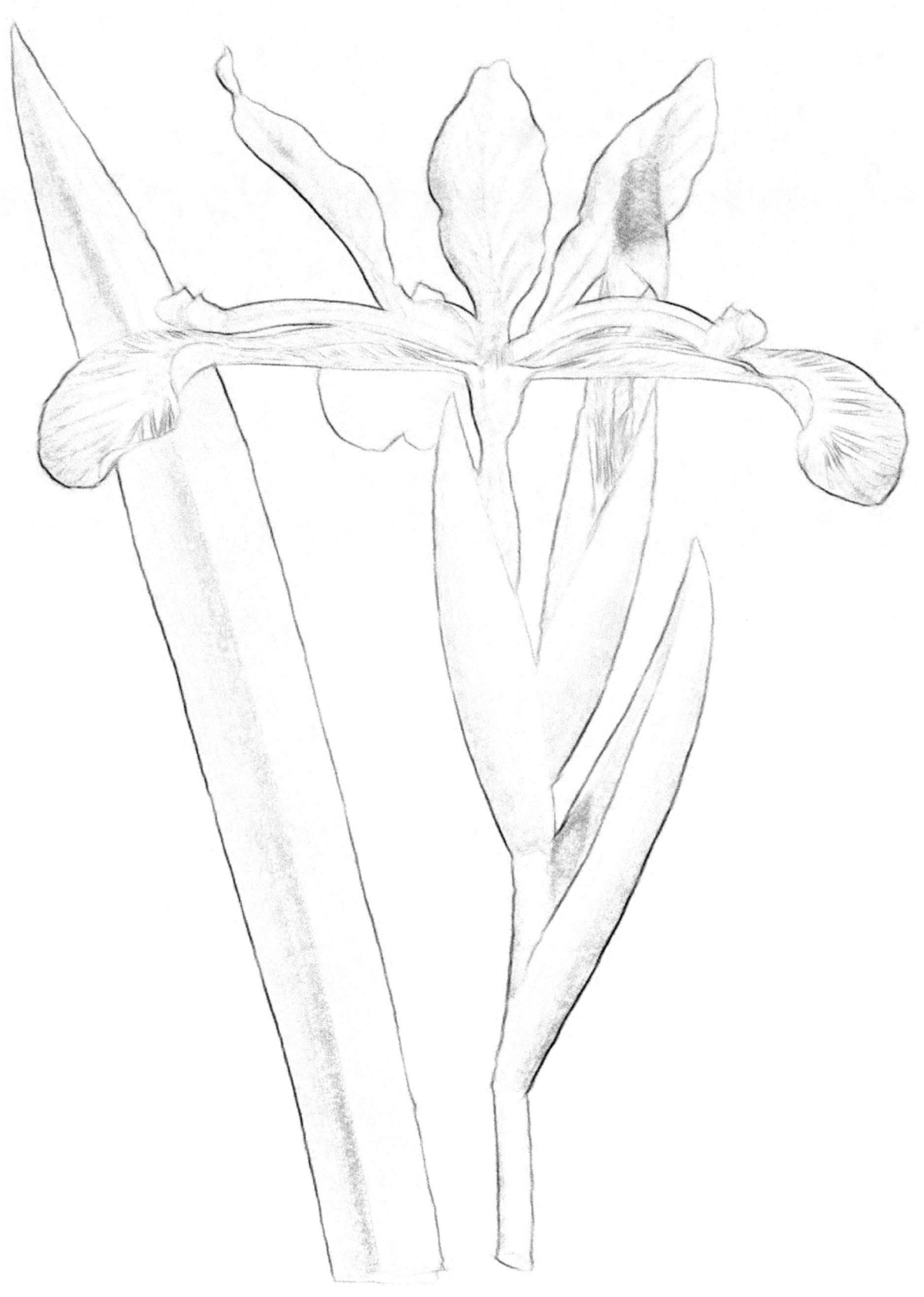

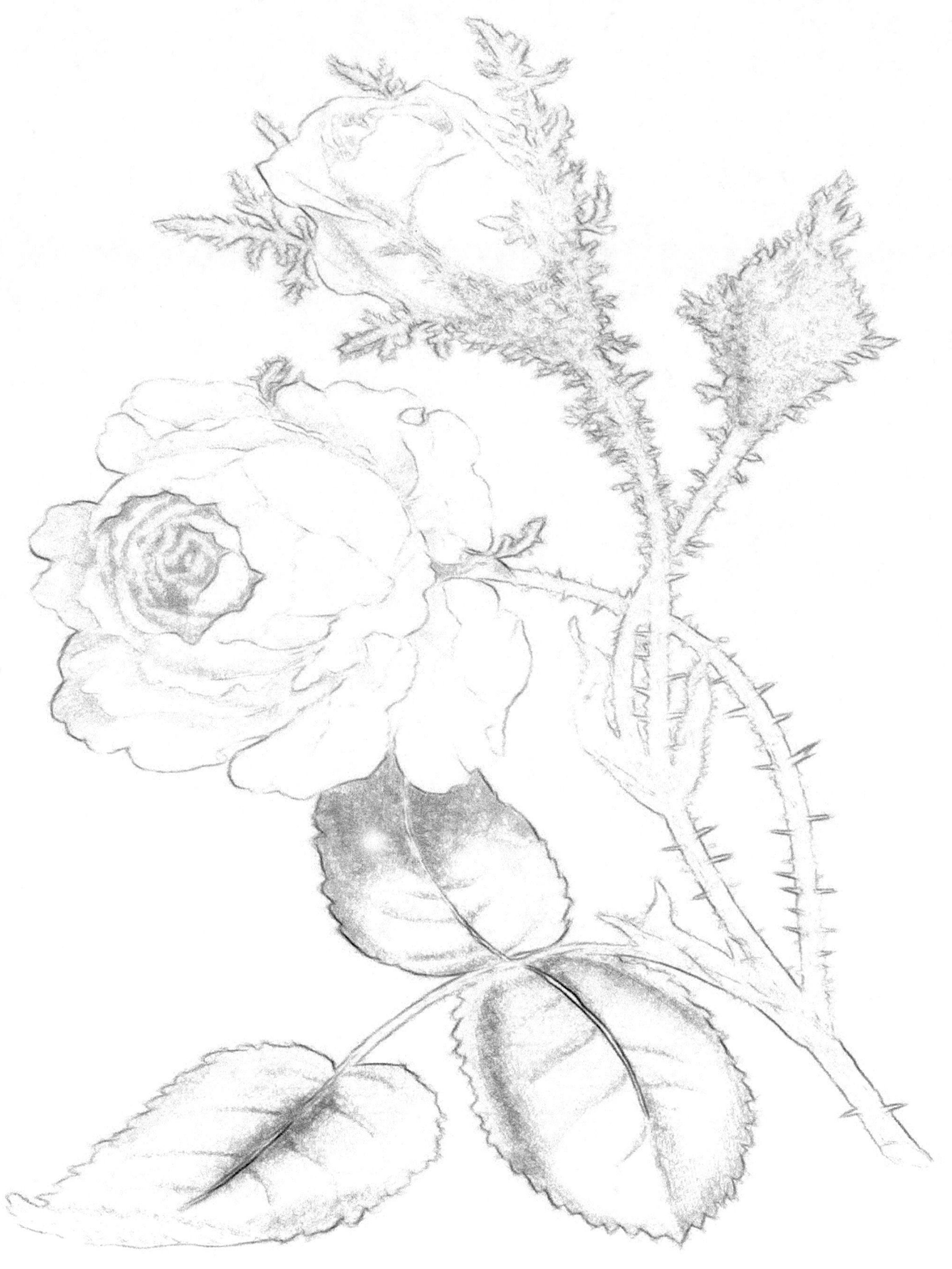

www.ingramcontent.com/pod-product-compliance
Lightning Source LLC
Chambersburg PA
CBHW080613180526
45168CB00007B/2897

* 9 7 8 1 5 1 1 8 8 1 1 9 7 *